T0394779

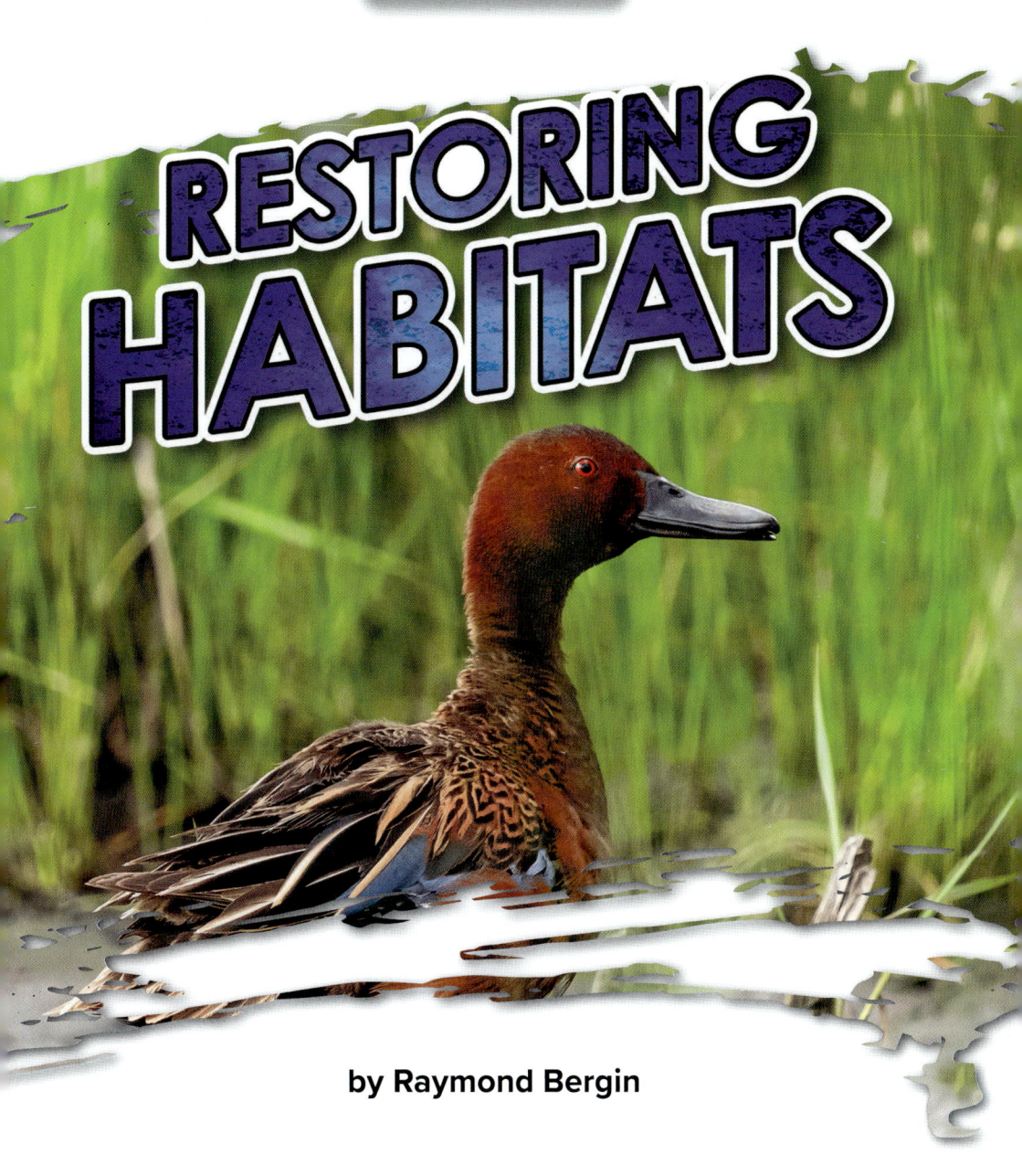

RESTORING HABITATS

by Raymond Bergin

BEARPORT
PUBLISHING

Minneapolis, Minnesota

Credits
Cover and title page, © Susan Hodgson/Adobe Stock; 4–5, © Jonathan Ross/Adobe Stock; 6, © faiz/Adobe Stock; 7TL, © the__lightwriter/Adobe Stock; 7TR, © Lars johansson/Adobe Stock; 7BL, © Miguel/Adobe Stock; 7BR, © somchairakin/Adobe Stock; 8–9, © ondrejprosicky/Adobe Stock; 10–11, © ftfoxfoto/Adobe Stock; 12–13, © Nico Smit/Adobe Stock; 13, © SKT Studio/Adobe Stock; 15, © Jon/Adobe Stock; 16–17, © dam/Adobe Stock; 19, © Kent Gilbert/Associated Press; 20–21, © Public domain/Wikimedia; 21, © PatrickZiegler/iStock; 23T, © Patrick M. Quigley; 23B, © Patrick M. Quigley; 24–25, © CQUniversity Australis; 26–27, © eakarat/Adobe Stock; 28, © Iriana Shiyan/Adobe Stock; 29TL, © Sheri FresonkeHarper/Adobe Stock; 29UML, © viperagp/Adobe Stock; 29ML, © Xyfen/Adobe Stock; 29LML, © AnnaStills/Adobe Stock; 29UML, © artsandra/Adobe Stock; 29BL, © DragonImages/Adobe Stock

Bearport Publishing Company Product Development Team
Publisher: Jen Jenson; Director of Product Development: Spencer Brinker; Managing Editor: Allison Juda; Editor: Cole Nelson; Associate Editor: Tiana Tran; Production Editor: Naomi Reich; Designer: Kim Jones; Designer: Kayla Eggert; Designer: Steve Scheluchin; Production Specialist: Owen Hamlin

Statement on Usage of Generative Artificial Intelligence
Bearport Publishing remains committed to publishing high-quality nonfiction books. Therefore, we restrict the use of generative AI to ensure accuracy of all text and visual components pertaining to a book's subject. See BearportPublishing.com for details.

Library of Congress Cataloging-in-Publication Data is available at www.loc.gov or upon request from the publisher.

ISBN: 979-8-89577-051-1 (hardcover)
ISBN: 979-8-89577-168-6 (ebook)

Contents

A Changing Landscape

The scent of the ocean breeze is covered by the smell of fresh paint at a new seaside resort. The buildings have replaced a marsh full of life. Down the road, a meadow that once overflowed with wildflowers and butterflies has been paved over with parking lots. Nearby, a forest has been reduced to stumps as logging trucks drive in and out. What on Earth is going on here, and how can we fix it?

Farming, construction, and other human activities have changed more than 70 percent of Earth's land.

Home Sweet Home

All around the world, plants and animals live in different habitats. These natural homes provide living things with everything they need to survive—shelter, water, food, and space.

Habitats vary widely. Deserts are dry, and polar regions tend to be cold. Forests, grasslands, and **aquatic** habitats all host different types of **vegetation**. Plants and animals are often uniquely **adapted** to life within their habitats. Generally, they cannot find everything they need in any other place.

Currently, there are about 6.5 million **species** of plants and animals on dry land. In addition, there are more than 140,000 species in fresh water. Another 2.2 million live in the oceans.

Habitat Harm

The species within a habitat support one another. In fact, habitats are often strongest when they have more species, or greater **biodiversity**. If a habitat's conditions change, it can spell danger for a wide variety of life. For example, if certain vegetation is removed, some plant-eaters may go hungry. They would have a harder time having young. Then, with fewer plant-eaters around, their predators could begin to starve. The chain reaction continues, impacting more and more life in an area. Human activities have caused many habitats to change or disappear completely.

Today, more than 46,300 species of plants and animals are at risk of dying off forever. Habitat loss is the main risk for 85 percent of the living things considered **threatened** or **endangered**.

Siberian tigers are endangered, but the animals are crucial to the health of their habitats.

Failing Forests

Forests are key habitats, supporting about 80 percent of land-based plants and animals on the planet. In the past, much of Earth was covered in forests. As human populations grew, however, they cut down trees. Forests with towering trees were taken down to make room for farms, towns, and roads. The wood was used as fuel and building materials.

Today, forest life is declining even further due to human activities. In fact, Earth is losing about 137 plant and animal species to **deforestation** every day.

Over the past 1,000 years, one third of the world's forests have disappeared. The land they grew on is an area about twice the size of the United States.

Disappearing Grasslands

Grasslands cover more than a third of the planet, yet they too are shrinking. Half of the world's grasslands have been lost. Many have been taken over by farms and ranches.

Cattle that roam across ranches on grasslands trample and eat vegetation that other creatures rely upon for food and shelter. Farmers often replace a wide variety of wild plants with just one or two kinds of crops. The decreased biodiversity creates a ripple effect across the habitat, supporting less and less life.

The **fertilizers** and **pesticides** that farmers use on crops can kill microorganisms, fungi, and insects in the soil. These **toxic** chemicals can also wash into waterways, harming aquatic life.

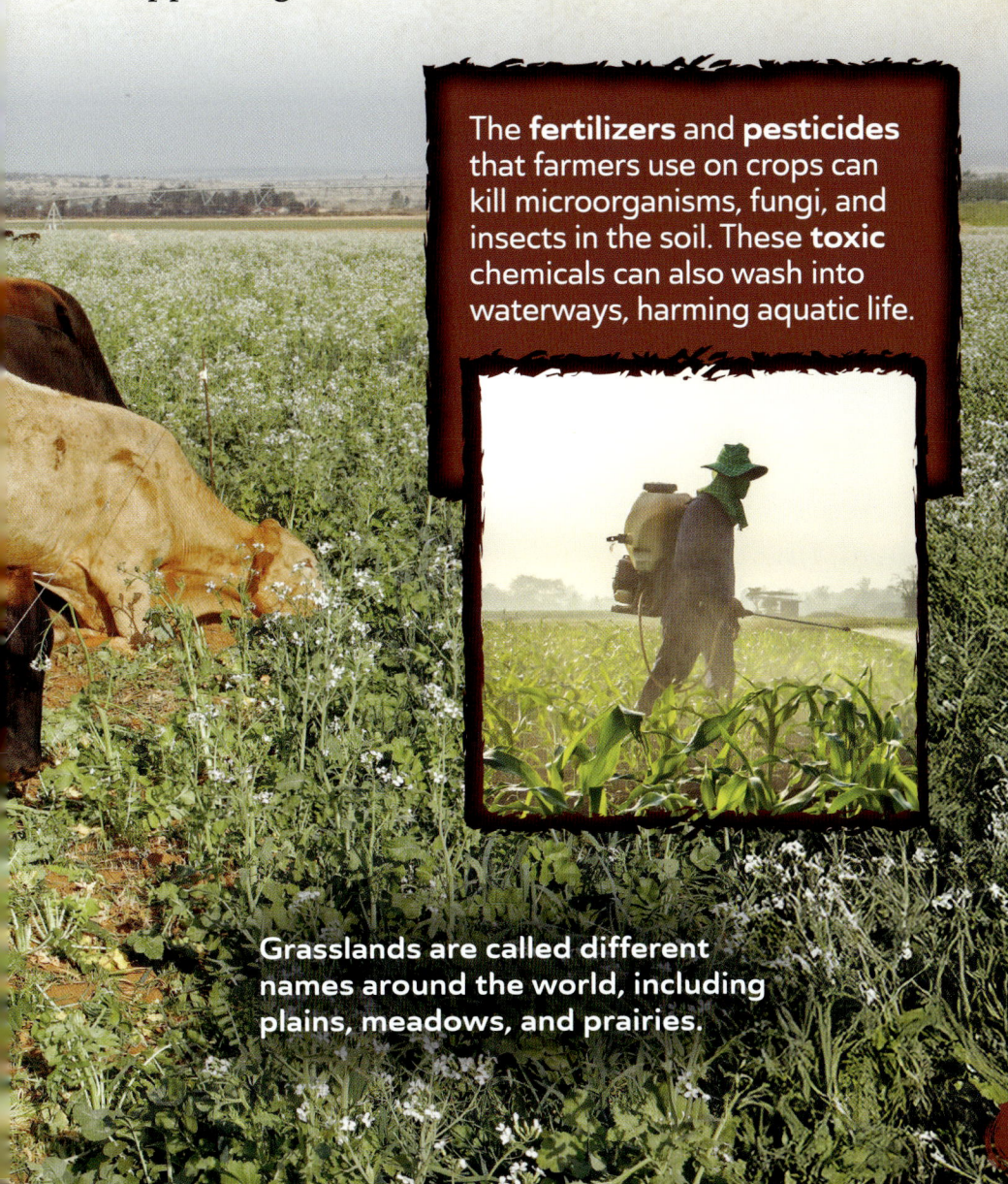

Grasslands are called different names around the world, including plains, meadows, and prairies.

Hanging Wetlands Out to Dry

Towns and cities change the natural landscape, with a heavy impact on coastal habitats. About 40 percent of the world's human population lives within 60 miles (100 km) of a coastline. This means many human structures are built along the water.

To make this **development** possible, **wetland** habitats between the land and sea are often drained, filled in, and built upon. Since 1970, more than one-third of the world's wetlands have been lost, threatening the species that rely on these habitats.

> Wetland plants absorb water, preventing coastal flooding during storms. Their loss becomes especially noticeable during strong hurricanes.

People have long built near water because it provides a steady food supply as well as a means of transportation.

No More Meadows

Human activity is also impacting oceans. Toxic waste washes from the land into the water. There, it joins **pollution** from oil spills and floating garbage. This impacts many ocean habitats, including seagrass meadows that grow in shallow coastal waters.

Many species of aquatic creatures spend at least part of their lives in seagrass meadows. The lush growth offers young animals hiding places from predators and protection from the force of waves and currents in the open water. The meadows' nutrient-rich leaves, flowers, and roots also feed many animals.

A single acre (0.4 ha) of seagrass can support more than 40,000 fish and 50 million invertebrates. Sadly, however, about a football field's worth of seagrass disappears every half hour.

Seagrass meadows are sometimes thought of as nature's nurseries because of all the young life they support.

Reforesting Costa Rica
The PES Program

While many habitats are stressed, plenty of people are stepping up to help. At one time, 75 percent of Costa Rica was covered by rainforests. But by 1987, almost half of the forests had been replaced by farms and ranches. The country's government swung into action. It banned cutting down trees without permission. In addition, its Payments for Environmental Services (PES) program paid landowners to help. Costa Ricans get government funding to replant **native** trees, clean waterways, and slow development. After nearly 40 years, more than half of Costa Rica is once again covered in forests.

Costa Rica's forests provide food and shelter for half a million plant and animal species. The wildlife includes 300,000 insect species, 800 kinds of birds, and 650 mammal species.

Costa Ricans young and old have helped replant the country's trees.

Protecting the Potholes
The Prairie Pothole Joint Venture

The Prairie Pothole Region of North America was one of the world's largest grassland-wetland habitats—until it shrunk by half. Stretching across the upper Midwest and Canada, a huge part of this area has been cleared and drained to make way for farming and ranching.

The Prairie Pothole Joint Venture is working to help restore the damaged habitat. It is a partnership between governments, environmental organizations, and landowners. The venture is replanting native grasses and wetland vegetation. It is also encouraging ranchers to consistently move livestock, allowing grasses to regrow while the animals graze elsewhere.

The Prairie Pothole Region is sometimes known as the duck factory. More than 10 million ducks and geese pass through it each spring. They make nests and feed in the habitat.

The region's namesake marshy potholes were formed by glaciers digging into the dirt during the last ice age.

Marsh Madness
The Upper Barataria Marsh Creation Project

In 2010, the Deepwater Horizon oil spill devastated wetlands along Louisiana's Gulf Coast. Many aquatic plants and animals died, and even more were left without a healthy home.

The National Oceanic and Atmospheric Administration (NOAA) took action to restore this wetland habitat. After extensive research, they launched the Upper Barataria Marsh Creation Project in 2018. This project began by pumping sediment to damaged areas to form a rich soil for marsh grass seeds to be planted. As the seeds grew, the wetlands began to reform. Today, these vital habitats once again provide food and shelter to millions of wetland creatures.

After the Deepwater Horizon oil platform exploded in 2010, about 134 million gallons (507 million L) of oil entered the gulf. This was the largest marine oil spill in history.

Upper Barataria Marsh
January 2023

Sediment for this project came from the Mississippi River. It was pumped 13 miles (21 km) to its new location.

Upper Barataria Marsh
August 2023

The newly created marshland stretches across 1,200 acres (490 ha).

Seedling Saviors
The Great Barrier Reef Foundation

Australia's Great Barrier Reef contains the world's largest seagrass meadows, accounting for 11 percent of the planet's seagrass. But the habitat is rapidly declining, due in part to pollution washing into the water from land.

The Great Barrier Reef Foundation is seeking to restore this important habitat. The organization is collecting healthy seagrass and growing its seeds in a land-based nursery. When the grass is ready, the Foundation transplants it into damaged meadows to give the areas new life.

In addition to providing food and shelter, seagrass meadows keep marine habitats healthy. The plant life traps and filters pollution in the water.

In total, the Foundation plans to grow and plant more than 1 million seeds to restore seagrass meadows.

Habitat Heroes

Life on Earth is in danger. The planet is experiencing rapid habitat loss. One-quarter of all plant and animal species face **extinction** if something isn't done. But people everywhere are taking action to help.

Scientists, environmental organizations, and governments are working hard to restore damaged habitats. They are cutting back on development and nurturing native life. With a little human assistance, newly restored habitats can thrive once again. Together, we can save our Earth!

In 2022, 190 countries adopted the Kunming-Montreal Global Biodiversity Framework. This plan seeks to conserve 30 percent of the world's land, inland water, and ocean areas.

Restore Habitats!

You don't have to look far to find habitats you can begin protecting today. The world just outside your window is full of habitats. Small steps can help these natural homes that support the health of the environment.

Create a backyard that supports wildlife. Grow native plants to provide food and shelter for little creatures.

Do not use fertilizers, pesticides, or insecticides on your yard.

Keep your outdoor spaces clear of pet waste, trash, and vehicle oils. These things can wash into storm drains and end up in aquatic habitats.

Recycle paper whenever possible. This means fewer trees have to be cut down for new paper.

Ask your school to consider growing native plants and putting up bird houses.

Participate in local replanting restoration projects, or take part in habitat cleanup days.

Glossary

adapted changed over time to be fit for the environment

aquatic related to water

biodiversity the existence of many different kinds of plants and animals in an environment

deforestation the cutting down and clearing of forests

development the use of land for human activity, commonly including building new construction

endangered at risk of becoming extinct in the near future

extinction when a type of animal or plant dies out completely

fertilizers substances added to soil to make plants grow better

native originally from and living in a particular place

pesticides chemicals that kill insects and other pests that damage crops

pollution harmful materials that make the land, air, or water dirty

species groups that animals are divided into, according to similar characteristics

threatened having an uncertain chance of surviving

toxic poisonous and potentially deadly

vegetation plant life

wetland an area of land, such as a marsh or swamp, where soil is usually covered by shallow water

Read More

Bergin, Raymond. *Forest Life Connections (Life on Earth! Biodiversity Explained).* Minneapolis: Bearport Publishing, 2023.

Buckey, A. W. *Land Preservation (Protecting Our Planet).* Minneapolis: ABDO Publishing, 2025.

Harris, Beatrice. *Jobs in Environmental Science (Inside Guide: STEM Careers).* New York: Cavendish Square Publishing, 2024.

Leatherland, Noah. *Wild Nature (Going Wild).* Minneapolis: Bearport Publishing, 2025.

Learn More Online

1. Go to **FactSurfer.com** or scan the QR code below.
2. Enter "**Restoring Habitats**" into the search box.
3. Click on the cover of this book to see a list of websites.

Index

About the Author

Raymond Bergin is a writer who lives in New Jersey and Massachusetts. He spends a lot of time trying to create a healthy and supportive habitat in his yard by planting trees, gardening, composting, and setting up bird houses.